CANINE LIBRAR

PEDIGREE DOGS IN (

BOOK TWO

GUNDOGS

*Official Standards
and
Colour Illustrations*

OTHER TITLES AVAILABLE
OR IN PREPARATION

PEDIGREE DOGS IN COLOUR

BOOK TWO

GUNDOGS

Roy Hodrien

Official Standards

*Colour Illustrations by
the Author*

NIMROD PRESS LTD

Dedicated to the memory of
Nan and Charlie

First Published in 1990

Pedigree Dogs in Colour   ISBN 1 85259 094 7

Book One – Hounds   ISBN 1 85259 205 2
Book Two – Gundogs   ISBN 1 85259 206 0
Book Three – Terriers   ISBN 1 85259 207 9
Book Four – Utility Group   ISBN 1 85259 208 7
Book Five – Working Group   ISBN 1 85259 209 5
Book Six – Toy Group   ISBN 1 85259 210 9

NIMROD PRESS LTD
15 The Maltings
Turk Street
Alton, Hants, GU34 1DL

Produced by Jamesway Graphics
Middleton, Manchester

Printed in England

CONTENTS

BOOK THREE – **TERRIERS**

BOOK FOUR – **UTILITY GROUP**

BOOK FIVE – **WORKING GROUP**

BOOK SIX – **TOY GROUP**

ACKNOWLEDGEMENTS

My thanks are offered to all those who assisted with this book. In particular I acknowledge the role of the British Kennel Club who gave permission for the *Official Standards* to be reproduced. The American Club also kindly allowed me to quote from their *Standards* showing the main variations from the British Standards.

ROY HODRIEN

PEDIGREE DOGS IN COLOUR

BOOK TWO

GUNDOGS

This is Book Two in a volume consisting
of six books each dealing with a main
group of dogs. The page numbering
follows that used in the main volume.

ENGLISH SETTER

Of the three setters in Britain, the **English** is in the middle in the popularity stakes. Many would argue, though, that he is the most balanced dog of the three, being strong and efficient in the field and affectionate as a companion.

He descends from an ancient spaniel-type although accurate information on his exact beginnings does not exist. What is certain is that the excellent dogs we know today owe much of their refinement to a Mr. Edward Laverack who began expert selective breeding in the early nineteenth century. By the 1850's Laverack's work reached fruition and English Setters began to appear in the show ring. As well as now being a much esteemed gun dog and pet in Britain, he is also well established in the U.S.A.

The English Setter makes a marvellous house dog for someone with a reasonable amount of room and plenty of time to devote to him. With children his behaviour is impeccable and he loves to join in with whatever is going on around him. Obviously his working background demands that he has plenty of free running, varied exercise.

The attractive coat requires plenty of regular brushing and the Engish Setter always looks better if the feathering on the legs is kept free from matting or tangling.

KEY TO CHARACTER	
INTELLIGENCE	****
TEMPERAMENT	*****
EASE OF COAT CARE	**
SUITABILITY FOR SMALL DWELLING	*
***** (5) = VERY GOOD	

BRITISH KENNEL CLUB STANDARD

ENGLISH SETTER

CHARACTERISTICS. — An intensely friendly and quiet-natured dog with a keen game sense.

GENERAL APPEARANCE. — Of medium height, clean in outline, elegant in appearance and movement.

Head and Skull. — Head should be long and reasonably lean, with a well-defined stop. The skull oval from ear to ear, showing plenty of brain room, and with a well-defined occipital protuberance. The muzzle moderately deep and fairly square; from the stop to the point of the nose should equal the length of skull from occiput to eyes; the nostrils wide and the jaws of nearly equal length; flews not to be too pendulous; the colour of the nose should be black or liver, according to the colour of the coat.

Eyes. — The eyes should be bright, mild and intelligent, and of a dark haze colour, the darker the better.

Ears. — The ears of moderate length, set on low, and hanging in neat folds close to the cheek; the tip should be velvety, the upper part clothed in fine silky hair.

Mouth. — The jaws should be strong, with a perfect regular and complete scissor bite, i.e., the upper teeth closely overlapping the lower teeth and set square to the jaws.

Neck. — Neck should be rather long, muscular and lean, slightly arched at the crest, and clean cut where it joins the head; towards the shoulder it should be larger and very muscular, not throaty or pendulous below the throat, but elegant in appearance.

Forequarters. — The shoulders should be well set back or oblique; the chest should be deep in the brisket, and of good depth and width between the shoulder blades. The forearm big and very muscular, with rounded bone, and the elbow well let down, Pasterns short, muscular, round and straight.

Body. — The body should be of moderate length, the back short and level with good round widely-sprung ribs and deep in the back ribs, i.e., well ribbed up.

Hindquarters. — The loins should be wide, slightly arched, strong and muscular, with defined second thigh. Stifles well bent and rugged, thighs long from hip to hock.

Feet. — The feet should be set on almost in line with the back; medium length, not curly or ropy, to be slightly curved or scimitar-shaped but with no tendency to turn upwards; the flag or feather hanging in long pendant flakes. The feather should not commence at the root, but slightly below, and increase in length to the middle, then gradually taper off towards the end; the hair long, bright, soft and silky, wavy, but not curly.

Coat. — The coat from the back of the head in a line with the ears ought to be slightly wavy, long and silky, which should be the case with the coat generally; the breeches and forelegs, nearly down to the feet, should be well feathered.

Colour. — The colour may be either black and white, lemon and white, liver and white or tricolour — that is black, white and tan; those without heavy patches of colour on the body, but flecked all over, preferred.

Weight and Size. — Height: Dogs 65 to 68cm (25½″ to 27″). Bitches 61 to 65cm (24″ to 25½″). Weight: Dogs 27 to 30Kg (60 to 66 lbs). Bitches 25 to 28Kg (55 to 61½ lbs).

Faults. — Any departure from the foregoing points should be considered a fault and the seriousness with which the fault is regarded should be in exact proportion to its degree.

Note. — Male animals should have two apparently normal testicles fully descended into the scrotum.

MAIN AMERICAN KENNEL CLUB VARIATION TO STANDARD FOR THE ENGLISH SETTER —

Height. — Dogs about 25 inches; bitches about 24 inches.

ENGLISH SETTER REGISTRATIONS 1981 — 87 INCLUSIVE

1981 — 1246
1982 — 1013
1983 — 1248
1984 — 1205
1985 — 1166
1986 — 1019
1987 — 1027

CRUFTS BEST-IN-SHOW WINNER TWICE.

1964 SH.CH. SILBURY SOAMES OF MADAVALE — MRS. A. WILLIAMS
1977 BOURNEHOUSE DANCING MASTER — MR. G.F. WILLIAMS

English Setter

German Short-Haired Pointer

GERMAN SHORTHAIRED POINTER

This breed has been described as the ultimate gundog and it is difficult to dispute this statement.

Developed with typical German thoroughness from the Spanish Pointer, English Foxhound and German Pointer-types, he possesses all that a sporting dog could require. The early specimens were a little heavier and coarser than today's dogs and it was the use of English Pointers which added the finishing touch, increasing intelligence and athleticism.

In the field his pointing ability is held in the highest regard and he is totally at home in water or on land when retrieving. He is extremely obedient and has a fine nose. The length of a hunt is of no consequence to the German Shorthaired Pointer as he has boundless stamina.

In the showring he can be an impressive sight and his even temperament makes the handler's job a fairly simple one. His sleek good looks and often striking markings have ensured his place as a firm favourite in dog shows across the world.

Unlike some truly sporting breds, the German Shorthaired Pointer blends very easily into a family home. Provided that exercise is lengthy and frequent and that the house and garden are of a fair size, he can make a marvellous pet. He revels in the company of children and is an effective and forceful guard.

KEY TO CHARACTER	
INTELLIGENCE	****
TEMPERAMENT	*****
EASE OF COAT CARE	*****
SUITABILITY FOR SMALL DWELLING	*
***** (5) = VERY GOOD	

BRITISH KENNEL CLUB STANDARD

GERMAN SHORTHAIRED POINTER

CHARACTERISTICS. — The German Shorthaired Pointer is a dual-purpose Pointer-Retriever and this accounts for his excellence in the field, which requires a very keen nose, perseverance in searching, and enterprise. His style attracts attention; he is equally good on land and in water, is biddable, an extremely keen worker, and very loyal.

GENERAL APPEARANCE. — A noble, steady dog showing power, endurance and speed, giving the immediate impression of an alert and energetic (not nervous) dog whose movements are well co-ordinated. Neither unduly small nor conspicuously large, but of medium size, and like the hunter, "With a short back stand over plenty of ground". Grace of outline, clean cut head, sloping long shoulders, deep chest, short back and powerful hindquarters, good bone composition, adequate muscle, well carried tail and taut coat giving a thoroughbred appearance.

Head and skull. — Clean-cut, neither to light nor too heavy, but well proportioned to the body. The skull sufficiently broad and slightly rounded. The furrow between the eyes not so deep, and the occiput not so pronounced as in the English Pointer. The nasal bone rises gradually from nose to forehead (this is more pronounced in the male) and should never possess a definite stop as in the English Pointer, but when viewed from the side there is a well defined stop effect due to the position of the eyebrows. The lips fall away almost vertically from a somewhat protruding nose and continue in a slight curve to the corner of the mouth. Lips well developed but not over hung. Jaws powerful and sufficiently long to enable the dog to pick up and carry game. Dish-faced and snipy muzzle are not desirable. Nose solid brown, wide nostrils well opened and soft.

Eyes. — Medium size, soft and intelligent, not protruding nor too deep set. Varying in shades of brown to tone with coat. Light eye not desirable. Eyelids should close properly.

Ears. — Broad and set high; neither too fleshy nor too thin with a short soft coat; hung close to the head, no pronounced fold, rounded at the tip and should reach almost to the corner of the mouth when brought forward.

Gordon Setter

Hungarian Vizsla

Mouth. — Teeth sound and strong. Molar teeth meeting exactly and the eyeteeth should fit close in a true scissor bite. Neither overshot nor undershot.

Neck. — Moderately long, muscular and slightly arched, becoming larger towards the shoulders. Skin should not fit too closely.

Forequarters. — Shoulder sloping and very muscular with top of shoulder blades close; upper arm bones between shoulder and elbow long. Elbows well laid back, neither pointing outwards nor inwards. Forelegs straight and lean, sufficiently muscular and strong but not coarse-boned. Pasterns slightly sloping, almost straight but not quite.

Body. — Chest must appear deep rather than wide but not out of proportion to the rest of the body; ribs deep and well sprung, never barrel-shaped nor flat as in the hound; back ribs reaching well down to tucked up loins. Chest measurement immediately behind the elbows smaller than about a hands-breadth behind the elbows, so that the upper arm has freedom of movement. Firm, short back, not arched. The loin wide and slightly arched; the croup wide and sufficiently long, neither too heavy nor too sloping starting on a level with the back and sloping gradually towards the tail. Bones solid and strong not clumsy and porous.

Hindquarters. — The hips broad and wide falling slightly towards the tail. thighs strong and well muscled. Stifles well bent. Hocks square with the body and slightly bent, turning neither in nor out. Pasterns nearly upright.

Feet. — Compact, close-knit, round to spoon shaped, well padded, should turn neither in nor out. Toes well arched and heavily nailed.

Tail. — Starts high and thick growing gradually thinner. Docked to medium length by two-fifths to half its length. When quiet tail should be carried down and when moving horizontally, never held high over the back or bent.

Coat. — Skin should not fit loosely or fold. Coat short, flat and coarse to the touch, slightly longer under the tail.

Colour. — Solid liver, liver and white spotted, liver and white spotted and ticked, liver and white ticked, black and white.

Weight and Size. — Dogs 25 to 31.8Kg (55 to 70 lbs), bitches 20.4 to 27.2Kg (45 to 60 lbs). Size — dogs 58 to 64cm (23″ to 25″) and bitches 53 to 59cm (21″ to 23″) at the shoulder, Symmetry is most essential.

Faults. — Bone structure too clumsy, sway-back, head too large, deep wrinkles in forehead, cone-shaped skull or occiput too prominent. Ears too long or too closely set together, eye-lids not closing properly. Wrinkles in neck. Feet or elbows turned inwards or outwards. Soft, sunken or splayed toes; cowhocks, straight hindlegs, or down on pasterns. Tail starting too low, undocked, too thick, curled up or too furry. Tri-coloured.

Note. — Male animals should have two apparently normal testicles fully descended into the scrotum.

GERMAN SHORTHAIRED POINTER REGISTRATIONS 1981 — 87 INCLUSIVE

1981 — 850
1982 — 629
1983 — 829
1984 — 740
1985 — 780
1986 — 916
1987 — 710

YET TO WIN CRUFTS BEST-IN-SHOW.

Irish Setter
Pointer

Curly-Coated Retriever

Flat-Coated Retriever

GORDON SETTER

The Gordon Setter has his beginnings about two hundred years ago and is named after his founder, the fourth Duke of Gordon. The Kennels of Gordon Castle were known to have produced setters of varying colours, some black and tan, some black and white and some black, white and tan. Several other breeders of the time used the esteemed dogs of the Duke in their kennels with some slight variations resulting. Many people have varying views on exactly which breeds were introduced to the early Gordon Setter's blood to arrive at the standardised version. The Collie, Pointer, Field Spaniel, Bloodhound and Irish Setter have all been mentioned as possibilities. It seems likely that the Irish Setter, at least, is responsible for the superb, rich mahogony markings, with the occasional all red Gordon Setter still appearing. The black and tan coloured dogs were always the most popular and today no other colour is acceptable.

The Gordon Setter is the largest and hardiest setter with excellent stamina and recuperative powers, an immense asset in the eyes of the shooting enthusiast. Although he does not possess the speed of his lighter relatives, he is more stable and dependable.

He should not be taken on lightly as a pet, as he is a sporting dog first and foremost and will expect plenty of free running. This is not to say that he is difficult to get along with, quite the opposite being true, but an owner should never keep the Gordon Setter in "cooped up" conditions.

KEY TO CHARACTER	
INTELLIGENCE	****
TEMPERAMENT	****
EASE OF COAT CARE	**
SUITABILITY FOR SMALL DWELLING	*
***** (5) = VERY GOOD	

BRITISH KENNEL CLUB STANDARD

GORDON SETTER

GENERAL APPEARANCE. — A stylish dog, built on galloping lines, having a thoroughbred appearance consistent with its build which can be compared to a weight carrying hunter. Must have symmetrical conformation throughout, showing true balance. Strong, fairly short and level back. Shortish tail. Head fairly long, clearly lined and with intelligent expression, clear colours and long flat coat.

Head and Skull. — Head deep rather than broad, but definitely broader than the muzzle, showing brain room. Skull slightly rounded and broadest between the ears. The head should have a clearly indicated stop and length from occiput to stop should be slightly longer than from stop to nose. Below and above the eyes should be lean and the cheeks as narrow as the leanness of the head allows. The muzzle should be fairly long with almost parallel lines and not pointed, as seen from above or from the side. The flews not pendulous but with clearly indicated lips. Nose big and broad, with open nostrils and black in colour. The muzzle should not be quite as deep as its length.

Eyes. — Of fair size, not too deep not too prominent but sufficiently under the brows to show keen and intelligent expression. Dark brown and bright.

Ears. — Set low on the head and lying close to it, of medium size and thin.

Mouth. — Must be even and not under nor overshot.

Neck. — Long, lean and arched to the head and without any throatiness.

Forequarters. — Shoulders should be long and slope well back; with wide flat bone and fairly close at withers; should not be loaded, i.e., too thick, which interferes with liberty of movement. Elbows well let down and showing well under the body, which gives freedom of action. Forelegs big, flat-boned and straight, with strong upright pasterns, well feathered.

Body. — Of moderate length, deep in brisket, with ribs well sprung. Deep in back ribs, i.e., well-ribbed up. Loins wide and slightly arched. Chest not too broad.

Hindquarters. — Hind legs from hip to hock should be long, broad and muscular; hock to heel short and strong, stifles well bent; hocks straight, not inclined either in or out. Pelvis should tend to the horizontal, i.e., opposite of goose rump.

Feet. — Oval, with close knit, well-arched toes, with plenty of hair between. Full toe pads and deep heel cushions.

Tail. — Fairly short, straight or slightly scimitar shaped and should not reach below the hocks. Carried horizontal or below line of back. Thick at the root tapering to a fine point. The feather or flat which starts near the root should be long and straight, and growing shorter uniformly to the point.

Coat. — On the head and front of legs and tips of ears should be short and fine, but on the other parts of the body and legs it ought to be of moderate length, fairly flat and free as possible from curl or wave. The feather on the upper portion of the ears should be long and silky, on the back of the hind legs long and fine; a fair amount of hair on the belly forming a nice fringe which may extend on chest and throat. All feathering to be as flat and straight as possible.

Colour. — Deep shining coal-black, with no sign of rustiness, with tan markings of a rich chestnut red, i.e., colour of a ripe horse-chestnut as taken from shell. Tan should be lustrous. Black pencilling allowed on toes and also black streak under jaw. *Tan markings:* two clear spots over the eyes not over threequarters of an inch in diameter. On the sides of the muzzle, the tan should not reach above the base of nose, resembling a stripe around the end of the muzzle from one side to the other. On the throat. Two large clear spots on the chest. On the inside of the hind legs and inside the thighs showing down the front of the stifle and broadening out to the outside of the hind legs from the hock to the toes. It must, however, not completely eliminate the black on the back of the hind legs. On the forelegs, up to the elbows behind, and to the knees or a little above, in front. Around the vent. A white spot on chest is allowed but the smaller the better.

Weight and Size. — As a guide to size, shoulder height for males 66cm (26″) and weight about 29.5Kg (65 lbs). Females, 62cm (24½″) and weight about 25.4Kg (56 lbs). In show condition.

Faults. — General Impression: unintelligent appearance. The bloodhound type with heavy and big head and ears and clumsy body; the collie type with pointed muzzle and curved tail. The Head: pointed, snipy, down or upturned muzzle, too small or large mouth. The Eyes: too light in colour, too deep set or too prominent. The Ears: set too high, or unusually broad or heavy. The Neck: thick and short. Shoulders and Back: irregularly formed. The Chest: too broad. The Legs and Feet: crooked legs. Outturned elbows. The toes scattered, flat footed. The Tail: too long, badly carried or hooked at the end. The Coat: curly, like wool, not shining. The Colour: yellow, or straw-coloured tan, or without clearly defined lines between the different colours. White feet. Too much white on the chest. In the black there should be no tan hairs.

Note. — Male animals should have two apparently normal testicles fully descended into the scrotum.

MAIN AMERICAN KENNEL CLUB VARIATION TO STANDARD FOR THE GORDON SETTER —

Size. — Shoulder height for males, 24 to 27 inches. For females, 23 to 26 inches.

Weight. — Males, 55 to 80 pounds; females, 45 to 70 pounds.

GORDON SETTER REGISTRATIONS 1981 — 87 INCLUSIVE

1981 — 529
1982 — 501
1983 — 478
1984 — 575
1985 — 586
1986 — 528
1987 — 456

YET TO WIN CRUFTS BEST-IN-SHOW.

HUNGARIAN VIZSLA

Although it is not certain that the Vizsla was first bred in Hungary, there is little doubt that it is there that all the major refinements of this first class sporting dog have been developed.

During the prosperous days of the Austro-Hungarian empire, the Vizsla was used to hunt boar and deer amongst other prey. The well-to-do noblemen of the time wanted a fit, efficient dog that could be easily trained to all the sportsman's needs. The selective breeding pursued by these huntsmen was largely responsible for the form anc character of today's Vizsla. He has been kept as one of the purest of breeds which is not surprising as his ability in the field could scarcely have been improved upon by out-crossing.

As a family pet the Hungarian Vizsla is to be highly recommended. His temperament is unwavering with all age groups and his cleanliness and easy management make him a desirable member of any household.

Training is no problem and the beautiful russet gold coat requires only minimal attention.

Exercise should be lengthy and frequent, lovers of the outdoors being ideal owners.

```
┌─────────────────────────────────────────────────────────────┐
│                     KEY TO CHARACTER                          │
├─────────────────────────────────────────────────────────────┤
│  INTELLIGENCE                          ****                   │
│                                                               │
│  TEMPERAMENT                           *****                  │
│                                                               │
│  EASE OF COAT CARE                     *****                  │
│                                                               │
│  SUITABILITY FOR                        *                     │
│  SMALL DWELLING                                               │
├─────────────────────────────────────────────────────────────┤
│                 ***** (5) = VERY GOOD                         │
└─────────────────────────────────────────────────────────────┘
```

BRITISH KENNEL CLUB STANDARD

HUNGARIAN VIZSLA

CHARACTERISTICS. — The Hungarian Vizsla should be lively and intelligent, obedient but sensitive, very affectionate and easily trained. It was bred for hunting for fur and feather on open ground or in thick cover, pointing and retrieving from both land and water.

GENERAL APPEARANCE. — A medium sized dog of distinguished appearance, robust and not too heavily boned.

Head and Skull. — The head should be gaunt and noble. The skull should be moderately wide between the ears with a median line down the forehead and a moderate stop. The muzzle should be a little longer than the skull and although tapering should be well squared at the end. The nostrils should be well developed, broad and wide. The jaws strong and powerful. The lips should cover the jaws completely and should be neither loose nor pendulous. The nose should be brown.

Eyes. — Neither deep nor prominent, of medium size, being a shade darker in colour than the coat. The shape of the eyes should be slightly oval and the eyelids should fit tightly. A yellow or black eye is objectionable.

Ears. — The ears should be moderately low set, proportionately long with a thin skin and hang down close to the cheeks, should be rounded 'V' shaped not fleshy.

Mouth. — Sound white teeth meeting in a scissor bite, full dentition is desirable.

Forequarters. — Shoulders should be well laid and muscular, elbow straight pointing neither in nor out, the forearm should be long.

Body. — Back should be level, short well muscled, withers high. The chest should be moderately broad and deep with prominent breast bone. The distance from the withers to the lowest part of the chest should be equal to the distance from the chest to the ground. The ribs should be well sprung and the belly should be tight with a slight tuck-up beneath the loin. The croup should be well muscled.

Hindquarters. — Should be straight when viewed from the rear, the thighs should be well developed with moderate angulation, the hocks well let down.

Feet. — Rounded with toes short, arched and well closed. A cat like foot is desirable, hare foot is objectionable. Nails short, strong and a shade darker in colour than coat, dew claws should be removed.

Gait. — Graceful and elegant with a lively trot and ground covering gallop.

Tail. — Should be of moderate thickness, rather low set, with one third docked off. Whilst moving should be held horizontally.

Coat. — Should be short and straight, dense and coarse and feel greasy to the touch.

Colour. — Russet gold. Small white marks on chest and feet, though acceptable, are not desirable.

Weight and Size. — Optimum Weight — 22 to 30Kg (48½ to 66 lbs). Height at withers — Dogs 57 to 64cm (22½" to 25") Bitches 53 to 60cm (21" to 23½").

Faults. — Any departure from the foregoing points should be considered a fault and the seriousness of the fault should be in exact proportion to its degree.

Note. — Male animals should have two apparently normal testicles fully descended into the scrotum.

MAIN AMERICAN KENNEL CLUB VARIATION TO STANDARD FOR THE HUNGARIAN VIZSLA —

Known in the U.S.A. as simply the Vizsla or the Hungarian Pointer.

Size. — The idal male is 22 to 24 inches at the highest point over the shoulder blades. The ideal female is 21 to 23 inches.

HUNGARIAN VIZSLA REGISTATIONS 1981 — 87 INCLUSIVE

1981 — 153
1982 — 173
1983 — 136
1984 — 226
1985 — 236
1986 — 225
1987 — 169

YET TO WIN CRUFTS BEST-IN-SHOW.

IRISH SETTER

This, the most popular of the Setters, was developed in Ireland in the mid-nineteenth century using Spaniels, Pointers and Setter-type dogs. Unfortunately it is impossible to ascertain exactly which combintions of breeds were used, but since the Irish Setter's official classification in 1876, he has remained a very pure-bred dog.

Surprising as it may seem to modern dog lovers who are familiar with the consistent solid red colour of these dogs, the earliest Irish Setters were mainly white with red patches. Being mainly a dog used for vigorous work in the field, appearance was secondary to physical durability and intelligence, therefore any coat colour was accepted. But eventually, as the breed began to make inroads into the show world, the fashion began to be for self-coloured red dogs. Although even to this day, some white is permissible, anything approaching a large area of white is undesirable.

As a gun dog he has a fine track record, showing great speed, agility and a keen nose. In recent years, the working side to his nature has somewhat taken a back seat to his need for beauty. Some would regard this as unfortunate, but it is also easy to see why the Irish Setter is in such demand as a show dog. When well presented he is a dog of great elegance and of course the coat always demands the onlooker's attention.

Training both for the gun and for the home can prove a little difficult at first, but with perseverance he will become responsive and loyal. He is a dog of very high spirits and natural friendliness so plenty of human attention and exercise are vital.

KEY TO CHARACTER	
INTELLIGENCE	****
TEMPERAMENT	****
EASE OF COAT CARE	**
SUITABILITY FOR SMALL DWELLING	*
***** (5) = VERY GOOD	

BRITISH KENNEL CLUB STANDARD

IRISH SETTER

GENERAL APPEARANCE. — Must be racey, full of quality, and kindly in expression.

Head and Skull. — The head should be long and lean, not narrow or snipy, and not coarse at the ears. The skull oval (from ear to ear), having plenty of brain room, and with well-defined occipital protuberance. Brows raised, showing stop. The muzzle moderately deep, and fairly square at end. From the stop to the point of the nose should be long, the nostrils wide, and the jaws of nearly equal length, flews not to be pendulous. The colour of the nose: dark mahogany, or dark walnut, or black.

Eyes. — Should be dark hazel or dark brown and ought not to be too large.

Ears. — The ears should be of moderate size, fine in texture, set on low, well back; and hanging in a neat fold close to the head.

Mouth. — Not over or undershot.

Neck. — Should be moderately long, very muscular, but not too thick, slightly arched, free from all tendency to throatiness.

Forequarters. — The shoulders to be fine at the points, deep and sloping well back. The chest as deep as possible, rather narrow in front. The fore legs should be straight and sinewy, having plenty of bone, with elbows free, well let down, not inclined either in or out.

Body. — Should be proportionate, the ribs well sprung, leaving plenty of lung room. Loins muscular, slightly arched.

Hindquarters. — Should be wide and powerful. The hind legs from hip to hock should be long and muscular; from hock to heel short and strong. The stifle and hock joints well bent, and not inclined either in or out.

Feet. — Should be small, very firm, toes strong, close together and arched.

Tail. — Should be of moderate length, proportionate to the size of the body, set on rather low, strong at root, and tapering to a fine point; to be carried as nearly as possible on a level with or below the back.

Coat and Feathering. — On the head, front of the legs, and tips of the ears, should be short and fine, but on all other parts of the body and legs it ought to be of moderate length, flat, and as free as possible from curl or wave. The feather on the upper portion of the ears should be long and silky; on the back of fore and hind legs should be long and fine; a fair amount of hair on the belly forming a nice fringe, which may extend on chest and throat. Feet to be well feathered between the toes. Tail to have a nice fringe of moderately long hair, decreasing in length as it approaches the point. All feathering to be as straight and as flat as possible.

Colour. — The colour should be rich chestnut, with no trace whatever of black; white on chest, throat, chin or toes, or a small star on the forehead, or a narrow streak or blaze on the nose or face not to disqualify.

Note. — Male animals should have two apparently normal testicles fully descended into the scrotum.

MAIN AMERICAN KENNEL CLUB VARIATION TO STANDARD FOR THE IRISH SETTER —

Size. — Twenty-seven inches at the withers and a show weight of about 70 pounds is considered ideal for a dog; the bitch 25 inches, 60 pounds.

IRISH SETTER REGISTRATIONS 1981 — 87 INCLUSIVE

1981 — 3122
1982 — 2675
1983 — 2450
1984 — 1997
1985 — 1938
1986 — 1790
1987 — 1529

CRUFTS BEST-IN-SHOW WINNER 1981.
CH. ASTLEY'S PORTIA OF RUA — MR. AND MISS TUITE.

POINTER

This lean, athletic gun dog breed has it's beginnings in Europe. It is thought that British soldiers returning from war in Spain in the early 18th century brought a strain of Spanish pointing dog home with them. The breed was very successful with the shooting fraternity of the time, but eventually the demanding English sportsmen felt they needed a faster breed. This was laboriously acheived through selective breeding, until the Pointer we know now was established in 1800. The idea of crossing the Pointer with the Foxhound was dabbled with, but it was thought that this lessened the ability to "point" out the game and that it made the breed a little unruly.

It should always be remembered by the Pointer owner that his dog was specifically bred for speed and stamina. Therefore, every effort should be made to provide plenty of running exercise, a walk "around the block" being inadequate. If allowed to use his boundless energy in this way, then his naturally sociable and even temperament will shine through.

A well cared for Pointer is a regal, graceful animal, and is to be highly recommended to a conscientious owner.

KEY TO CHARACTER	
INTELLIGENCE	****
TEMPERAMENT	*****
EASE OF COAT CARE	*****
SUITABILITY FOR SMALL DWELLING	*
***** (5) = VERY GOOD	

BRITISH KENNEL CLUB STANDARD

POINTER

CHARACTERISTICS. — The Pointer should be symmetrical and well built all over. Alert, with the appearance of strength, endurance and speed.

Head and Skull. — The skull should be medium breadth and in proportion to the length of fore-face; the stop well defined, pronounced occipital bone. Nose and eye-rims dark, but may be lighter in the case of a lemon and white-coloured dog. The nostrils wide, soft and moist. The muzzle somewhat concave, and ending on a level with the nostrils, giving a slightly dish-faced appearance. The cheek-bones should not be prominent. Well developed soft lip.

Eyes. — The same distance form the occiput as from the nostrils. A slight depression under the eyes, which should be bright and kindly in expression, not bold or staring, and not looking down the nose. The colour of the eyes either hazel or brown according to the colour of the coat.

Mouth. — Scissors bite, neither under nor overshot.

Neck. — Long, muscular, slightly arched, springing cleanly from the shoulders and free from throatiness.

Ears. — The ears should be set on fairly high, and lie close to the head, they should be of medium length, and inclined to be pointed at the tips.

Forequarters. — The shoulders long, sloping, and well laid back. The chest just wide enough for plenty of heart room. The brisket well let down, to a level with the elbows. The fore-legs straight and firm, of good oval bone, with the back sinews strong and visible. The knee joint should be flat with the front of the leg, and protrude very little on the inside. Pasterns lengthy, strong and resilient.

Body. — Well-sprung ribs, gradually falling away at the loin, which should be strong, muscular and slightly arched. The couplings short. The haunch bones well spaced and prominent, but not above the level of the back. The general outline from head to tail being a series of graceful curves, giving a strong but lissom appearance.

Hindquarters. — Well turned stifles. The hock should be well let down, and cose to the ground. A good expanse of thigh, which should be very muscular, as should also the second-thighs.

Feet. — The feet oval, with well-knit, arched toes, well cushioned underneath.

Gait. — Smooth, covering plenty of ground with each stride. Driving hind action, elbows neither turning in nor out. Definitely not a hackney action.

Tail. — The tail of medium length, thick at the root, growing gradually thinner to the point. It should be well covered with close hair, and carried on a level with the back, with no upward curl. With the dog in movement the tail should lash from side to side.

Coat. — The coat should be fine, short, hard and evenly distributed, perfectly smooth and straight, with a decided sheen.

Colour. — The usual colours are lemon and white, orange and white, liver and white, and black and white. Self colours and tricolours are also correct.

Size. — Desirable heights. Dogs 63 to 69cm (25″ to 27″). Bitches 61 to 66cm (24″ to 26″).

Note. — Male animals should have two apparently normnal testicles fully descended into the scrotum.

MAIN AMERICAN KENNEL CLUB VARIATION TO STANDARD FOR THE POINTER —

Size. — Dogs; height 25″ to 28″, weight 55 to 75 pounds. Bitches; height 23″ to 26″, weight 45 to 65 pounds.

POINTER REGISTRATIONS 1981 –- 87 INCLUSIVE

1981 — 838
1982 — 737
1983 — 762
1984 — 737
1985 — 801
1986 — 626
1987 — 650

CRUFTS BEST-IN-SHOW WINNER TWICE.
1935 PENNINE PRIMA DONNA — A. EGGLESTON.
1958 CH. CHIMING BELLS — MRS. W. PARKINSON.

CURLY-COATED RETRIEVER

As can at once be seen in the coat of this fine breed, the Curly-Coated Retriever shares ancestry with the Poodle and the Irish Water Spaniel. All probably descend from the Water Dog which was common in Europe several centuries ago. Even when the Curly-Coated Retriever was established, it is believed that Poodle blood was re-introduced to the breed and this may have resulted in an even tighter curl to the coat.

This breed has always been highly regarded as a worker in the field and his great stamina and intelligence are well known. When working in water the dense curls of the coat are vitually water tight so cold conditions hold no fear for him. His coat also offers good protection when foraging in potentially hazardous undergrowth.

Although kept by relatively few people, the Curly-Coated Retriever has all the good points associated with retrievers. His temperament is very steady and all members of the family will receive his loyalty and affection. This devotion will be demonstrated when guarding the owner's house and his solid build makes him a force to be reckoned with.

A good deal of exercise is necessary for this essentially outdoor breed, with rural suroundings being preferred.

To maintain his striking appearance, the coat must never be brushed as this discourages the tight curling.

KEY TO CHARACTER	
INTELLIGENCE	****
TEMPERAMENT	*****
EASE OF COAT CARE	**
SUITABILITY FOR SMALL DWELLING	*
***** (5) = VERY GOOD	

BRITISH KENNEL CLUB STANDARD

RETRIEVER (CURLY-COATED)

GENERAL APPEARANCE. — A strong smart upstanding dog showing activity, endurance and intelligence.

Head and Skull. — Long, well proportioned flat skull, jaws strong and long but not inclined to snipiness. Nose black in the black-coated variety with wide nostrils, coarseness of head to be deprecated.

Eyes. — Black or brown but not "gooseberry" coloured, rather large but not too prominent.

Ears. — Rather small, set on low, lying close to the head and covered with short curls.

Mouth. — Teeth strong and level.

Neck. — Should be moderately long, free from throatiness.

Forequarters. — Shoulders should be very deep, muscular and well laid back.

Hindquarters. — Strong and muscular, hock low to the ground with good bend to stifle and hock.

Body. — Well sprung ribs, good depth of brisket, not too long in the loin, as little tucked-up in flank as possible.

Feet. — Round and compact with well-arched toes.

Gait. — Covering plenty of ground with drive.

Tail. — Moderately short, carried fairly straight and covered with curls, tapering towards the point, gay tail not desirable.

Coat. — Should be one mass of crisp small curls all over. This being the main characteristic of the breed should be given great consideration when making judging awards.

Colour. — Black or liver.

Size. — Desirable height at withers: Dogs 68.58cm (27″); Bitches 63.50cm (25″).

Faults. — Wide skull, light eyes, curled tail and bad movement.

Note. — Male animals should have two apparently normal testicles fully descended into the scrotum.

CURLY COATED RETRIEVER REGISTRATIONS 1981 — 87 INCLUSIVE

1981 —   90
1982 —   69
1983 — 100
1984 —   88
1985 — 114
1986 —   83
1987 — 135

YET TO WIN CRUFTS BEST-IN-SHOW.

FLAT-COATED RETRIEVER

The Flat-Coated Retriever has only been present in Britain since the late Nineteenth century and was originally known as the Wavy-Coated Retriever. The early dogs were rather unrefined and are though to have resulted from Labrador and Newfoundland crossings. Although evidence of these two breeds is still very visible in the Flat-Coated Retriever, modern specimens have been improved by the introduction of Collie and Setter blood. This helped to produce an agile dog with a flatter coat.

He is a highly-rated breed amongst the shooting fraternity having unsurpassed retrieving qualities and an ability to work well on land or in water, the latter skill no doubt reflecting his Newfoundland ancestry.

In the early part of this century, the Flat-Coated Retriever was a very popular breed in Britain and although his popularity is not at such a level today, he has a good size following and his future is assured.

He is a beautifully balanced dog in all respects. His physique is nicely proportional, strong but not heavy and his temperament is even and friendly. Like all retrievers he is of high intelligence and loves human company. A great deal of exercise is required by the Flat-Coated Retriever and an energetic owner who is keen on the outdoors would be ideal.

```
┌─────────────────────────────────────────────────────────┐
│                    KEY TO CHARACTER                      │
├─────────────────────────────────────────────────────────┤
│  INTELLIGENCE                    ****                     │
│                                                          │
│  TEMPERAMENT                     *****                    │
│                                                          │
│  EASE OF COAT CARE               ***                      │
│                                                          │
│  SUITABILITY FOR                 *                        │
│  SMALL DWELLING                                          │
├─────────────────────────────────────────────────────────┤
│              ***** (5) = VERY GOOD                       │
└─────────────────────────────────────────────────────────┘
```

BRITISH KENNEL CLUB STANDARD

RETRIEVER (FLAT-COATED)

GENERAL APPEARANCE. — A bright, active dog of medium size with an intelligent expression, showing power without lumber, and raciness without weediness.

Head and Skull. — The head should be long and nicely moulded. The skull flat and moderately broad. There should be a depression or stop between the eyes, slight and in no way accentuated, so as to avoid giving either a down or a dish-faced appearance. The nose of a good size, with open nostrils. The jaws should be long and strong, with a capacity of carrying a hare of pheasant.

Eyes. — Should be of medium size, dark-brown or hazel, with a very intelligent expression (a round, prominent eye is a disfigurement) and they should not be obliquely placed.

Ears. — Should be small and well set-on, close to the side of the head.

Neck. — the head should be well set in the neck, which latter should be long and free from throatiness, symmetrically set and obliquely placed in shoulders running well into the back to allow of easily seeking for the tail.

Forequarters. — The chest should be deep and fairly broad, with a well-defined brisket, on which the elbows should work cleanly and evenly. The legs are of the greatest importance, the forelegs should be perfectly straight, with bone of good quality carried right down to the feet and when the dog is in full coat the legs should be well feathered.

Body. — The fore-ribs should be fairly flat, showing a gradual spring and well-arched in the centre of the body, but rather lighter towards the quarters. Open couplings are to be ruthlessly condemned. The back should be short, square and well ribbed up.

Golden Retriever
Labrador Retriever

American Cocker Spaniel
Clumber Spaniel

Hindquarters. — Should be muscular. The stifle should not be too straight or too bent, and the dog must neither be cow-hocked nor move too widely behind; in fact he must stand and move true on legs and feet all round. The legs should be well feathered.

Feet. — Should be round and strong with toes close and well arched, the soles being thick and strong.

Gait. — Free and flowing, straight and true as seen from front and rear.

Tail. — Short, straight and well set on, carried gaily, but never much above the level of the back.

Coat. — Should be dense, of fine quality and texture, flat as possible.

Colour. — Black or liver.

Weight and Size. — Should be between 27.2 and 31.8Kg (60 to 70 lbs).

Note. — Male animals should have two apparently normal tesitcles fully descended into the scrotum.

MAIN AMERICAN KENNEL CLUB VARIATION TO STANDARD FOR THE FLAT-COATED RETRIEVER —

Size. — Preferred height is 23 to 24½ inches at the withers for dogs, 22 to 23½ for bitches.

FLAT-COATED RETRIEVER REGISTRATIONS 1981 — 87 INCLUSIVE

1981 — 667
1982 — 715
1983 — 818
1984 — 860
1985 — 992
1986 — 940
1987 — 971

CRUFTS BEST-IN-SHOW WINNER 1980.
CH. SHARGLEAM BLACKCAP — MISS P. CHAPMAN.

GOLDEN RETRIEVER

The origins of this magnificent breed are, as is so often the case, open to question. One popular theory has been that a certain Lord Tweedmouth developed the first Golden Retrievers from a group of yellow Russian circus dogs that were touring Britain in the mid-nineteenth century. Others believe he may have sprung from Flat-Coated Retriever stock with perhaps some out crossing with water spaniels.

However he came into being, there is no doubt that the Golden Retriever has been and still is one of the most complete dogs in the world. As a worker in the field his ability is beyond question. He learns very quickly and has the priceless asset of being able to use his own initiative. Stamina, strength and determination complete the picture of this true sportsman's dog.

Such is the intelligence and reliability of the Golden Retriever that he is one of the first choices as a guide dog for the blind, a task which we all see him perform so marvellously.

As a pet for a family with young children, he could not be recommended too highly. He seems incapable of any nastiness and will revel in human company and affection. But coupled with his placid nature is an ability to guard, something that is always appreciated in a family home.

A fair sized house and garden would suit a Golden Retriever best and lengthy and regular exercise sessions are very important.

Cocker Spaniel
English Springer Spaniel

Field Spaniel

KEY TO CHARACTER	
INTELLIGENCE	*****
TEMPERAMENT	*****
EASE OF COAT CARE	***
SUITABILITY FOR SMALL DWELLING	*
***** (5) = VERY GOOD	

BRITISH KENNEL CLUB STANDARD

RETRIEVER (GOLDEN)

GENERAL APPEARANCE. — Should be a symmetrical, active, powerful dog, a good level mover, sound and well put together, with a kindly expression, not clumsy nor long in the leg.

Head and Skull. — Broad skull, well set on a clean and muscular neck, muzzle powerful and wide, not weak-jawed, good stop.

Eyes. — Dark and set well apart, very kindly in expression, with dark rims.

Ears. — Well proportioned, of moderate size, and well set on.

Mouth. — Teeth should be sound and strong. Neither overshot nor undershot the lower teeth just behind but touching the upper.

Neck. The neck should be clean and muscular.

Forequarters. — The forelegs should be straight with good bone. Shoulders should be well laid back and long in the blade.

Body. — Well-balanced, short coupled, and deep through the heart. Ribs deep and well sprung.

Hindquarters. — The loins and legs should be strong and muscular, with good second thighs and well bent stifles. Hocks well let down, not cow-hocked.

Feet. — Round and cat-like, not open nor splay.

Tail. — Should not be carried too gay nor curled at the tip.

Coat. — Should be flat or wavy with good feathering, and dense, water-resisting undercoat.

Colour. — Any shade of gold or cream, but neither red nor mahogany. The presence of a few white hairs on chest permissible. White collar, feet, toes or blaze should be penalised. Nose should be black.

Weight and Size. — The average weight in good hard condition should be: Dogs, 32 to 37Kg (70 to 80 lbs); Bitches, 27 to 32Kg (60 to 70 lbs). Height at shoulder: Dogs 56 to 61cm (22″ to 24″); Bitches 51 to 56cm (20″ to 22″).

Note. — Male animals should have two apparently normal testicles fully descended into the scrotum.

MAIN AMERICAN KENNEL CLUB VARIATION TO STANDARD FOR THE GOLDEN RETRIEVER —

Size. — Males 23 to 24 inches in height at withers; Females 21½ to 22½ inches. Weight for dogs 65 to 75 pounds; bitches 55 to 65 pounds.

GOLDEN RETRIEVER REGISTRATIONS 1981 — 87 INCLUSIVE

$$1981 — 8837$$
$$1982 — 9702$$
$$1983 — 10270$$
$$1984 — 10448$$
$$1985 — 11451$$
$$1986 — 11948$$
$$1987 — 11290$$

YET TO WIN CRUFTS BEST-IN-SHOW.

Sussex Spaniel

Irish Water Spaniel

LABRADOR RETRIEVER

This excellent breed is now so numerous in this country that it is perhaps easy to forget that he has his origins thoudands of miles away in Newfoundland. These dogs were also to be found in Labrador but the first specimens to come to Britain were purchased from Newfoundland fishermen in the early nineteenth century. Their main function was to retrieve fish, a task they were perfectly suited to being strong, obedient and very much at home in the water.

There were two types of these dogs to be found in Newfoundland. One was very large with a thick, long coat and the other smaller with a smooth coat. They were both of similar conformation and when they first appeared in Britain they were both known as Newfoundlands. Later, though, the two were divided into the Labrador Retrievers and Newfoundlands we are now familiar with.

Ever since his standard was drawn up in 1916, the Labrador has been regarded as one of the finest gun dogs in the world. He is tireless and ultra efficient at all types of retrieving and still has a great affinity with water work.

The Labrador is blessed with extreme intelligence and this coupled with the most genial nature has made him a natural choice for that most complicated and important of tasks, guiding the blind.

If sufficient space is available then this breed is without fault as a pet. He has the patience and good humour to cope with teasing children and is a rewarding companion at all times. Plenty of exercise is very important and overfeeding must always be avoided.

KEY TO CHARACTER	
INTELLIGENCE	*****
TEMPERAMENT	*****
EASE OF COAT CARE	*****
SUITABILITY FOR SMALL DWELLING	*
***** (5) = VERY GOOD	

BRITISH KENNEL CLUB STANDARD

RETRIEVER (LABRADOR)

GENERAL APPEARANCE. — The general appearance of the Labrador should be that of a strongly-built, short-coupled, very active dog, broad in the skull, broad and deep through the chest and ribs, broad and strong over the loins and hindquarters. The coat close, short with dense undercoat and free from feather. The dog must move neither too wide nor too close in front or behind, he must stand and move true all round on legs and feet.

Head and Skull. — The skull should be broad with a pronounced stop so that the skull is not in a straight line with the nose. The head should be clean cut without fleshy cheeks. The jaws should be medium length and powerful and free from snipiness. The nose wide and the nostrils well developed.

Eyes. — The eyes of medium size expressing intelligence and good temper, should be brown or hazel.

Ears. — Should not be large and heavy and should hang close to the head, and set rather far back.

Mouth. — Teeth should be sound and strong. The lower teeth just behind but touching the upper.

Neck. — Should be clean, strong and powerful and set into well placed shoulders.

Forequarters. — The shoulders should be long and sloping. The forelegs well boned and straight from the shoulder to the ground when viewed from either the front or side. The dog must move neither too wide nor too close in front.

Body. — The chest must be of good width and depth with well-sprung ribs. The back should be short coupled.

Weimaraner

Welsh Springer Spaniel

Hindquarters. — The loins must be wide and strong with well-turned stifles; hindquarters well developed and not sloping to the tail. The hocks should be slightly bent and the dog must neither be cow-hocked nor move too wide or too close behind.

Feet. — Should be round and compact with well-arched toes and well-developed pads.

Tail. — The tail is a distinctive feature of the breed; it should be very thick towards the base, gradually tapering towards the tip, of medium length and practically free from any feathering, but clothed thickly all round with the Labrador's short, thick dense coat, thus giving that peculiar "rounded" appearance which has been described as the "Otter" tail. The tail may be carried gaily, but should not curl over the back.

Coat. — The coat is another distinctive feature of the breed, it should be short and dense and without wave with a weather-resisting undercoat and should give a fairly hard feeling to the hand.

Colour. — The colour is generally black or yellow — but other whole colours are permitted. The coat should be free from any white markings but a small white spot on the chest is allowable. The coat should be of a whole colour and not of a flecked appearance.

Weight and Size. — Desired height for Dogs, 56 to 57cm (22″ to 22½″); Bitches 54 to 56cm (21½″ to 22″).

Faults. — Under or overshot mouth; no undercoat; bad action; feathering; snipiness on the head; large or heavy ears; cow-hocked; tail curled over back.

Note. — Male animals should have two apparently normal testicles fully descended into the scrotum.

MAIN AMERICAN KENNEL CLUB VARIATION TO STANDARD FOR THE LABRADOR RETRIEVER —

Weight and Size. — Approximate weight of dogs and bitches in working condition: Dogs 60 to 70 pounds; Bitches 55 to 70 pounds. Height at shoulders: Dogs 22½ to 24½ inches; Bitches 21½ to 23½ inches.

LABRADOR RETRIEVER REGISTRATIONS 1981 — 87 INCLUSIVE

1981 — 12543
1982 — 13488
1983 — 14016
1984 — 13681
1985 — 15156

CRUFTS BEST-IN SHOW WINNER 3 TIMES.

1932 BRAMSHAW BOB — LORNA COUNTESS HOWE
1933 BRAMSHAW BOB — LORNA COUNTESS HOWE
1937 CH. CHEVERALLA BEN OF BANCHORY — LORNA COUNTESS HOWE

AMERICAN COCKER SPANIEL

The American and English Cocker Spaniels of today are both descended from the smallest of the original British Spaniels. It seems that the specimens that crossed the Atlantic developed differently purely as a result of American preferences.

In the U.S.A. breeders retained the hunting instinct of the breed but since their dogs were bred smaller, their prey was normally such things as small birds. The American Cocker excels at this work for although not as robust as his English cousin, he is blessed with good stamina and willingness to learn.

Since his registration in Britain in 1968 he has been well received here but mainly for the showring or as a pet, rather than for field work. The American Cocker is a dog that shows well, and the thick long coat is shown at it's glorious best when the dog is on the move. Apart from the coat, the main feature that distinguishes the American from the English Cocker is the shorter, squarer muzzle.

He has no faults as a dog for a family home and will prove to be well-liked by all age groups. He can be house-trained very simply and can reach a high standard of obedience if the owner puts in enough work with him.

The American Cocker Spaniel will revel in as much exercise both inside and outside the home as the owner's family can provide, so he is a breed more suited to active types.

KEY TO CHARACTER	
INTELLIGENCE	****
TEMPERAMENT	****
EASE OF COAT CARE	*
SUITABILITY FOR SMALL DWELLING	***
***** (5) = VERY GOOD	

BRITISH KENNEL CLUB STANDARD

SPANIEL (AMERICAN COCKER)

GENERAL APPEARANCE. — A serviceable-looking dog with a refinedly chiselled head; standing on straight legs and well up at the shoulders; of compact body and wide, muscular quarters. The American Cocker Spaniel's sturdy body, powerful quarters and strong, well-boned legs show him to be a dog capable of considerable speed combined with great endurance. Above all he must be free and merry, sound well balanced throughout, and in action show a keen inclination to work, equable in temperament with no suggestion of timidity.

Head and Skull. — Well developed and rounded with no tendency towards flatness, or pronounced roundness, of the crown (dome). The forehead smooth, i.e., free from wrinkles, the eyebrows and stop clearly defined, the median line distinctly marked and gradually disappearing until lost rather more than halfway up to the crown. The bony structure surrounding the socket of the eye should be well chiselled; there should be no suggestion of fullness under the eyes nor prominence in the cheeks which, like the sides of the muzzle, should present a smooth, clean-cut appearance. To attain a well-proportioned head, which above all should be in balance with the rest of the dog, the distance from the tip of the nose to the stop at a line drawn across the top of the muzzle between the front corners of the eyes, should approximate one-half the distance from the stop at this point up over the crown to the base of the skull. The muzzle should be broad and deep, with square even jaws. The upper lid should be of sufficient depth to cover the lower jaw, presenting a square appearance. The nose of sufficient size to balance the muzzle and foreface, with well-developed nostrils and black in colour in the blacks and black-and-tans; in the reds, buffs, livers, and parti-colours and in the roans it may be black or brown, the darker colouring being preferable.

Mouth. — The teeth should be sound and regular and set at right angles to their respective jaws. The relation of the upper teeth to the lower should be that of scissors, with the inner surface of the upper in contact with the outer surface of the lower when the jaws are closed.

Eyes. — The eyeballs should be round and full and set in the surrounding tissue to look directly forward and give the eye a slightly almond-shape appearance. The eye should be neither weak nor goggled. The expression should be intelligent, alert, soft and appealing. The colour of the iris should be dark brown to black in the blacks, black and tans, buffs and creams, and in the darker shades of the parti-colours and roans. In the reds, dark hazel; in the livers, parti-colours, and roans of the lighter shades, not lighter than hazel, the darker the better.

Ears. — Lobular, set on a line no higher than the lower part of the eye, the leather fine and extending to the nostrils, well clothed with long, silky, straight or wavy hair.

Neck. — The neck sufficiently long to allow the nose to reach the ground easily, muscular and free from pendulous "throatiness". It should rise strongly from the shoulders and arch slightly as it tapers to join the head.

Forequarters. — The shoulders deep, clean-cut and sloping without protrusion and so set that the upper point of the withers are at an angle which permits a wide spring of rib. Forelegs straight, strongly boned and muscular and set close to the body well under the scapulae. The elbows well let down and turning neither in nor out. The pasterns short and strong.

Body. — Its height at the withers should approximate the length from the withers to the set-on of tail. The chest deep, its lowest point no higher than the elbows, its front sufficiently wide for adequate heart and lung space, yet not so wide as to interfere with straight forward movement of the forelegs. Ribs deep and well-sprung throughout. Body short in the couplings and flank, with its depth at the flank somewhat less than at the last rib. Back strong and sloping evenly and slightly downward from the withers to the set-on of tail. Hips wide with quarters well rounded and muscular. The body should appear short, compact and firmly knit together, giving the impression of strength.

Hindquarters. — The hind legs should be strongly boned and muscled with good angulation at the stifle and powerful, clearly defined thighs. The stifle joint should be strong and there should be no slippage in motion or when standing. The hocks should be strong, well let down and when viewed from behind, the hind legs should be parallel when in motion and at rest.

Feet. — Feet compact, not spreading, round and firm, with deep, strong, tough pads and hair between the toes; they should turn neither in nor out.

Gait. — The American Cocker Spaniel possesses a typical sporting dog gait. Prerequisite to good movement is balance between the fore and hind quarters. He drives with his strong powerful rear quarters and is properly constructed to the shoulder and forelegs so that he can reach forward without constriction in a full stride to counter balance the driving force of the rear. Above all, his gait is co-ordinated, smooth and effortless. The dog must cover ground with his action and excessive animation should never be mistaken for proper gait.

Tail. — The docked tail should be set on and carried on a line with the topline of the back, or slightly higher; never straight up like a terrier and never so low as to indicate timidity. When the dog is in motion the action should be merry.

Coat. — On the head, short and fine; on the body, medium length, with enough undercoating to give protection. The ears, chest, abdomen, and legs should be well feathered, but not so excessively as to hide the American Cocker Spaniel's true lines and movement or affect his appearance and function as a sporting dog. The texture is most important. The coat should be silky,flat or slightly wavy, and of a texture which permits easy care. Excessive or curly or cottony texture coat should be penalised.

Colour. — Black should be jet black; shadings of brown or liver in the sheen of the coat is not desirable. Black and Tan (classified under solid colours) should have definite tan markings on a jet black body. The tan markings should be distinct and plainly visible and the colour of the tan may be from the lightest cream to the darkest red colour. The amount of tan markings should be restricted to ten per cent or less of the colour of the specimen; tan markings in excess of ten per cent should be penalised. Tan markings which are not readily visible in the ring or the absence of tan markings in any of the specified locations should be penalised. The tan markings should be located as follows:-

1. A clear spot over each eye.
2. On the sides of the muzzle and on the cheeks.
3. On the underside of the ears.
4. On all feet and legs.
5. Under the tail.
6. On the chest, optional, presence or absence should not be penalised.

Tan on the muzzle which extends upwards over and joins should be penalised.

Any solid colour other than black should be of uniform shade. Lighter colouring of the feathering is permissible.

In all the above solid colours a small amount of white on chest and throat while not desirable, is allowed, but white in any other location should be penalised.

Parti-colours. Two or more definite colours appearing in clearly defined markings are essential. Primary colour which is ninety per cent or more should be penalised; secondary colour or colours which are limtied solely to one location should also be penalised. Roans are classified as parti-colours and may be of any of the usual roaning patterns. Tri-colours are any of the above colours combined with tan markings. It is preferable that the tan markings be located in the same pattern as for Black and Tan.

Size. — The ideal height at the withers for an adult dog is 38cm (15″) and for an adult bitch 35cm (14″). Height may vary 1.3cm (half an inch) above or below this ideal. A dog whose height exceeds 39cm (15½″) or a bitch whose height exceeds 37cm (14½″) should be penalised. An adult dog whose height is less than 37cm (14½″) or an adult bitch whose height is less than 34cm (13½″) should be penalised. Note: Height is determined by a line perpendicular to the ground from the top of the shoulder blades, the dog standing naturally with its forelegs and the lower hind legs parallel to the line of the measurement.

Note. — Male animals should have two apparently normal testicles fully descended into the scrotum.

AMERICAN COCKER SPANIEL REGISTRATIONS 1981 — 87 INCLUSIVE

1981 — 459
1982 — 462
1983 — 409
1984 — 405
1985 — 481
1986 — 367
1987 — 385

YET TO WIN CRUFTS BEST-IN-SHOW.

CLUMBER SPANIEL

The very early history of this heavyweight of the Spaniel family is very unclear, but it is known that the French Duc de Noailles presented several specimens of the Clumber Spaniel type to the Duke of Newcastle some 200 years ago. It is thought that the Duc de Noailles had probably possessed spaniels of the Cocker or Springer type and had crossed them with heavier breeds. When these dogs were received by the Duke of Newcastle, they were named after his home which was Clumber Park.

Since his introduction to Britain he has changed very little, having long been used as a successful shooting dog. The Clumber has an excellent nose and thorough appraoch to his work and although far from speedy he can move his bulk with surprising athleticism. His stamina is beyond question and he has been used as a good retriever and beater.

If taken as a pet, it should be remembered that like many heavy dogs the Clumber can tend towards laziness and obesity if not exercised sufficiently. He will prefer the country life, but will tolerate town living if he is given plenty of runs in parks or fields.

Providing an owner's home is of a fair size, he will make a fine family dog. He is no trouble to train and as his benign facial expression would suggest, has a commendable temperament.

KEY TO CHARACTER	
INTELLIGENCE	****
TEMPERAMENT	*****
EASE OF COAT CARE	***
SUITABILITY FOR SMALL DWELLING	*
***** (5) = VERY GOOD	

BRITISH KENNEL CLUB STANDARD

SPANIEL (CLUMBER)

GENERAL APPEARANCE — That of a dog with a thoughtful expression, very massive but active, which moves with a rolling gait characteristic of the breed.

Head and Skull. — Head large, square and massive, of medium length, broad on top, with a decided occiput; heavy brows with a deep stop; heavy muzzle, with well-developed flew, and level jaw and mouth. Nose square and flesh-coloured.

Eyes. — Dark amber, slightly sunk with some haw showing.

Ears. — Large, vine-leaf shaped, and well covered with straight hair, and hanging slightly forward, the feather not to extend below the leather.

Mouth. — Should be level and neither over nor undershot.

Neck. — Fairly long, thick and powerful, and well feathered underneath.

Forequarters. — Shoulders strong, sloping and muscular; chest deep. Legs short, straight, thick and strong.

Body. — Long and heavy, and near the ground, with well-sprung ribs. Back straight, broad and long.

Hindquarters. — Very powerful and well developed. Loin powerful, well let down in flank. Hocks low, stifles well bent and set straight.

Feet. — Large and round, well covered with hair.

Tail. — Set low, well feathered, and carried about level with the back.

Coat. — Abundant, close, silky, and straight; legs well feathered.

Colour. — Plain white, with lemon markings, orange permissible; slight head markings and freckled muzzle, with white body preferred.

Weight and Size. — Dogs about 25 to 31.8Kg (55 to 70 lbs); Bitches about 20.4 to 27.2Kg (45 to 60 lbs).

Nots. — Male animals should have two apparently normal testicles fully descended into the scrotum.

MAIN AMERICAN KENNEL CLUB VARIATION TO STANDARD FOR THE CLUMBER SPANIEL —

Height and Weight. — Males weigh between 70 and 85 pounds, bitches between 55 and 70 pounds. Males are about 19 to 20 inches at the withers, bitches are about 17 to 19 inches at the withers.

CLUMBER SPANIEL REGISTRATIONS 1981 — 87 INCLUSIVE

1981 —   57
1982 — 113
1983 — 111
1984 — 156
1985 — 199
1986 — 143
1987 —   97

YET TO WIN CRUFTS BEST-IN-SHOW.

COCKER SPANIEL

The Cocker Spaniel is well established as one of Britain's most popular breeds. He is an ideal size for most households and his marvellous personality and doleful facial expressions have won over many thousands of owners.

In the distant past, all English Spaniels were grouped together with no distinct categories such as Springer, Cocker and Sussex etc. It was in the early 19th century that the Cocker first emerged in his own right but it was some 100 years later that he was registered officially. The name "Cocker" derives from his use in woodcock shooting, where his size gives him an advantage over his larger relatives, in that he can penetrate dense undergrowth with greater ease. Whether it be woodcock, pheasant or other game, the Cocker is a prized sporting dog. Although he does not have the speed of setters or larger spaniels, he does have excellent stamina and scenting ability. The dense, wavy coat of the Cocker gives him efficient protection from the cold and can even help prevent minor injury when hunting in thorny conditions.

This breed can not be recommended highly enough to anyone seeking a faithful companion and affectionate pet. He is compatible with all age groups and does not require a great deal of room. Exercise, however is essential, for mild natured as he is, he can become bad tempered if bored and neglected.

KEY TO CHARACTER	
INTELLIGENCE	****
TEMPERAMENT	*****
EASE OF COAT CARE	***
SUITABILITY FOR SMALL DWELLING	***
***** (5) = VERY GOOD	

BRITISH KENNEL CLUB STANDARD

SPANIEL (COCKER)

GENERAL APPEARANCE. — That of a merry sturdy sporting dog. The Cocker Spaniel should be well balanced and compact and should measure about the same from the withers to the ground as from the withers to the root of the tail.

Head and Skull. — There should be a good square muzzle with a distinct stop which should be mid way between the tip of the nose and the occiput. The skull should be well developed, cleanly chiselled, neither too fine nor too coarse. The cheek bones should not be prominent. The nose should be sufficiently wide to allow for the acute scenting power of this breed.

Eyes. — The eyes should be full but not prominent, brown or dark brown in colour but never light, with a general expression of intelligence and gentleness though decidely wide awake, bright and merry. The rims should be tight.

Ears. — Lobular, set on low, on a level with the eyes, with fine leathers which extend to but not beyond the top of the nose; well clothed with long silky hair which should be straight.

Mouth. — Jaws should be strong and teeth should have a scissor bite.

Neck. — Neck should be moderate in length, clean in throat, muscular and neatly set in fine sloping shoulders.

Forequarters. — The shoulders should be sloping and fine, the chest well developed and the brisket deep, neither too wide nor too narrow in front. The legs must be well boned, feathered and straight and should be sufficiently short for concentrated power but not too short to interfere with the tremendous exertions expected from this grand little sporting dog.

Body. — Body should be immensely strong and compact for the size and weight of the dog. The ribs should be well sprung behind the shoulder blades, the loin short wide and strong, with a firm topline gently sloping downwards to the tail.

Hindquarters. — Hindquarters should be wide, well rounded and very muscular. The legs must be well boned feathered above the hock with a good bend of stifle and short below the hock allowing for plenty of drive.

Feet. — Feet should be firm, thickly padded and catlike.

Tail. — Tail should be set on slightly lower than the line of the back; it must be merry, carried in line with the back and never cocked up. The tail should not be docked too long nor too short to interfere with its merry action.

Coat. — Flat and silky in texture, never wiry or wavy, with sufficient feather; not too profuse and never curly.

Colour. — Various. In self colours no white is allowed except on the chest.

Gait. — There should be true through action both for and aft, with great drive covering the ground well.

Weight and Size. — The weight should be about 12.7 to 14.5Kg (28 to 32 lbs). The height at the withers should be approximately 38 to 39cm (15″ to 15½″) for bitches and approximatly 39 to 41cm (15½″ to 16″) for dogs.

Faults. — Light bone; straight shoulder; flat ribs; unsound movement; weak hocks; weak pasterns; open or large feet; frown; small beady eyes; undershot or overshot mouth; uncertain or aggressive temperament.

Note. — Male animals should have two apparently normal testicles fully descended into the scrotum.

MAIN AMERICAN KENNEL CLUB VARIATION TO STANDARD FOR THE COCKER SPANIEL —

Known as the English Cocker Spaniel in the U.S.A.

Weight and Size. — Ideal heights at withers: Males, 16 to 17 inches; females 15 to 16 inches. The most desirable weights: Males, 28 to 34 pounds; . ·males 26 to 32 pounds.

COCKER SPANIEL REGISTRATIONS 1981 — 87 INCLUSIVE

1981 — 8009
1982 — 7697
1983 — 8064
1984 — 7573
1985 — 7619

CRUFTS BEST-IN-SHOW WINNER 6 TIMES.

1930 LUCKYSTAR OF WARE — H. S. LLOYD
1931 LUCKYSTAR OF WARE — H. S. LLOYD
1938 EXQUISITE MODEL OF WARE — H. S. LLOYD
1939 EXQUISITE MODEL OF WARE — H. S. LLOYD
1948 TRACEY WITCH OF WARE — H. S. LLOYD
1950 TRACEY WITCH OF WARE — H. S. LLOYD

ENGLISH SPRINGER SPANIEL

The English Springer Spaniel has existed in similar form since the very birth of British sporting Spaniels. On a broad basis, the early shorter-legged Spaniels evolved into the Cocker and the taller dogs became Springers. But the latter were once known as Norfolk Spaniels, the name arising from the Duke of Norfolk's involvement with the breed. This name, however, was changed in the early part of this century to his current title. The word 'Springer' refers to the 'springing' of game from the undergrowth into the view of the huntsman.

In Britain and also in the U.S.A. he remains a highly regarded sporting dog, particularly for his prowess at bird work. He is a tireless and speedy worker, not at all inconvenienced by even the foulest weather. Training is no problem with such an intelligent dog and he thoroughly enjoys coping with whatever his master asks of him.

Nowadays there are two very distinct types of Springer, the worker and the show dog. The working dog tends to be more compact and rugged and the show specimen taller and moulded on more aesthetic lines, whilst still maintaining some of his natural fitness.

He is a dog of undoubted beauty and has an excellent disposition to match. A springer is the epitome of loyalty and fits very well into a family environment. Definitely a dog for the active, long periods of exercise on and off the lead are a must.

KEY TO CHARACTER	
INTELLIGENCE	****
TEMPERAMENT	*****
EASE OF COAT CARE	***
SUITABILITY FOR SMALL DWELLING	*
***** (5) = VERY GOOD	

BRITISH KENNEL CLUB STANDARD

SPANIEL (ENGLISH SPRINGER)

CHARACTERISTICS. — The English Springer is the oldest of our Sporting Gundogs and the taproot from which all of our sporting land spaniels (Clumbers excepted) have been evolved. It was originally used for the purpose of finding and springing game for the net, falcon, or greyhound, but at the present time it is used entirely to find, flush, and retrieve game for the gun. The breed is of ancient and pure origin, and should be kept as such.

GENERAL APPEARANCE. — The general appearance of the modern Springer is that of a symmetrical, compact, strong, upstanding, merry and active dog, built for endurance and activity. He is the highest on the leg and raciest in build of all British land Spaniels.

Head and Skull. — The skull should be of medium length and fairly broad and slightly rounded, rising from the foreface, making a brow or stop, divided by a fluting between the eyes gradually dying away along the forehead towards the occiput bone, which should not be peaked. The cheeks should be flat, that is not rounded or full. The foreface should be of proportionate length to the skull, fairly broad and deep without being coarse, well chiselled below the eyes, fairly deep and square in flew, but not exaggerated to such an extent as would interfere with comfort when retrieving. Nostrils well developed.

Eyes. — The eyes should be neither too full nor too small but of medium size, not prominent nor sunken but well set in (not showing haw) of an alert, kind expression. A mouse-like eye without expression is objectionable, as also is a light eye. The colour should be dark hazel.

Ears. — The ears should be lobular in shape, set close to the head, of good length and width, but not exaggerated. The correct set should be in line with the eye.

Mouth. — The jaws should be strong, with a perfect regular and complete scissor bite, i.e., the upper teeth closely overlapping the lower teeth and set square to the jaws.

Neck. — The neck should be strong and muscular, of nice length and free from throatiness, well set in the shoulders, nicely arched and tapering towards the head — thus giving great activity and speed. A ewe neck is objectionable.

Forequarters. — The forelegs should be straight and nicely feathered, elbows set well to body and with proportionate substance to carry the body, strong flexible pasterns.

Body. — The body should be strong and of proportionate length, neither too long nor too short, the chest deep and well developed with plenty of heart and lung room, well sprung ribs, loin muscular and strong with slight arch, and well coupled, thighs broad and msucular and well developed.

Hindquarters. — The hindlegs should be well let down from hip to hocks. Stifles and hocks moderately bent, inclining neither inwards nor outwards. Coarseness of hocks objectionable.

Feet. — Feet tight, compact, and well rounded with strong full pads.

Gait. — The Springer's gait is strictly his own. His forelegs should swing straight forward from the shoulder, throwing the feet well forward in an easy and free manner. His hocks should drive well under his body, following in a line with the forelegs. At slow movements many Springers have a pacing stride typical of the breed.

Tail. — The stern should be low and never carried above the level of the back, well feathered and with a lively action.

Coat. — The coat should be close, straight, and weather resisting without being coarse.

Colour. — Any recognised Land Spaniel colour is acceptable, but liver and white black and white,or either of these colours with tan markings preferred.

Weight and Size. — The approximate height should be 51cm (20″). The approximate weight should be 22.7Kg (50 lbs).

Note. — Male animals should have two apparently normal testicles fully descended into the scrotum.

MAIN AMERICAN KENNEL CLUB VARIATION TO STANDARD FOR THE ENGLISH SPRINGER SPANIEL —

Size and Proportion. — The ideal shoulder height for dogs is 20 inches; for bitches, 19 inches. Weight is dependent on the dog's other dimensions: a 20 inch dog, well proportioned, in good condition should weigh about 49 to 55 pounds.

ENGLISH SPRINGER SPANIEL REGISTRATIONS 1981 — 87 INCLUSIVE

1981 — 7055
1982 — 6984
1983 — 6825
1984 — 6235
1985 — 6666
1986 — 6474

YET TO WIN CRUFTS BEST-IN-SHOW.   1987 — 5999

FIELD SPANIEL

This is a rare Spaniel that, in the past, has suffered severely at the hands of thoughtless breeders. Having originally been developed from Cocker and Springer Spaniels around 1880, a craze set in for low-slung, thick-legged dogs which got so out of hand as to almost kill the breed off. After much dedicated work, conscientious breeders gradually bred out this almost Basset Hound-like appearance to give the pleasing form of today's Field Spaniels. Whilst still far from being long in the leg, this breed has become very agile and is a first class worker in the field.

His even temperament and responsiveness to training make him suitable both for sporting endeavours and as a fine dog for the home. Although he should be given a great deal of exercise, it would be difficult to point out a fault in this breed to a prospective owner. He would probably be happiest in a rural environment, but his easy going nature enables him to cope with most situations. Children are safe in his company and he thrives on all human affection.

We can only hope that such a beautiful dog does not disappear from the scene, as has been threatened in the past, for there is probably no better spaniel.

KEY TO CHARACTER	
INTELLIGENCE	****
TEMPERAMENT	*****
EASE OF COAT CARE	***
SUITABILITY FOR SMALL DWELLING	**
***** (5) = VERY GOOD	

BRITISH KENNEL CLUB STANDARD

SPANIEL (FIELD SPRINGER)

GENERAL APPEARANCE. — That of a well-balanced, noble, upstanding, sporting dog; built for activity and endurance; a combination of beauty and utility; of unusual docility

Head and Skull. — The head should be characteristic as is that of the Bulldog or the Bloodhound; its very stamp and countenance should at once convey the impression of high breeding, character and nobility; skull well developed, with a distinct occipital protuberance, which gives the character alluded to; not too wide across the muzzle, long and lean, neither snipy nor squarely cut, and in profile curving gradually from nose to throat; lean beneath the eyes, a thickness here gives coarseness to the whole head. The great length of muzzle gives surface for the free development of the olfactory nerve, and thus secures the highest possible scenting powers. Nose, well developed, good with open nostrils.

Eyes. — Not too full, but not small, receding or overhung. The colour in all cases to match the coat and markings, except in livers which may be a light hazel. Grave in expression suggesting docility and intelligence and showing no haw.

Ears. — Moderately long and wide, sufficiently clad with nice Setter-like feather and set low. They should fall in graceful folds, the lower parts curling inwards and backwards.

Mouth. — The jaws should be strong, with a perfect regular and complete scissor bite, i.e., the upper teeth closely overlapping the lower teeth and set square to the jaws.

Neck. — Long, strong and muscular, so as to enable the dog to retrieve his game without undue fatigue.

Forequarters. — The shoulders should be long and sloping and well set back, thus giving great activity and speed. The foreleg should be of fairly good length, with straight, clean, flat bone and nicely feathered. Immense bone is not desirable.

Body. — Should be of moderate length, well ribbed up to a good strong loin, straight or slightly arched, never slack. The chest, deep and well developed, but not too round and wide. Back and loins very strong and muscular.

Hindquarters. — Strong and muscular. The stifles should be moderately bent and not twisted either in or out.

Feet. — Not too small, round with short, soft hair between the toes; good, strong pads.

Tail. — Well set on and carried low, if possible below the level of the back, in a straight line or with a slight downward inclination, never elevated above the back, and in action always kept low, nicely fringed with wavy feather of silky texture.

Coat. — Flat or slightly waved, and never curled, sufficiently dense to resist the weather and not too short. Silky in texture, glossy and refined without duffelness, curliness or wiriness. On the chest, under the belly and behind the legs, there should be abundant feather, but never too much, especially below the hocks, and that of the right sort — viz., Setter-like.

Colour. — The Field Spaniel should be a self-coloured dog, viz.: Black, Liver, Golden Liver, Mahogany Red, Roan; or any of these colours with Tan over the Eyes, on the Cheeks, Feet and Pasterns. Other colours, such as Black and White, Liver and White, Red or Orange and White, etc., while not debarring a dog, is a fault.

Weight and Size. — From about 16 to 23Kg (35 to 50½ lbs). Height: about 46cm (18″) at shoulder.

Faults. — Any departure from the foregoing points should be considered a fault and the seriousness with which the fault is regarded should be in exact proportion to its degree.

Note. — Male animals should have two aparently normal testicles fully descended into the scrotum.

FIELD SPANIEL REGISTRATIONS 1981 — 87 INCLUSIVE

1981 —	79
1982 —	86
1983 —	77
1984 —	83
1985 —	85
1986 —	127
1987 —	83

YET TO WIN CRUFTS BEST-IN-SHOW.

IRISH WATER SPANIEL

The Irish Water Spaniel owes the bulk of his development to an Irishman called Justin McCarthy, who established the breed in the mid nineteenth century. He probably used gundogs from Spain when working to perfect the breed, although exactly which ones is not certain. There had been other water spaniels in Ireland prior to this and McCarthy used selected specimens of these.

The coat of the Irish Water Spaniel is unique in the spaniel family. Some might say that the cascading curls on the head and ears give him a rather soft lap dog type of expression. But the truth is that he is probably the best wildfowling dog in existence, having all the necessary attributes of strength, stamina and intelligence. The dense coat is slightly oily, giving excellent waterproofing and insulation, so he will not waver if called to retrieve from the iciest water.

Training the Irish Water Spaniel in the home is not a great problem due to his great willingness to learn and responsiveness to human company. They are a breed of high spirits and might be a little overpowering for toddlers. Lots of free running exercise is essential so an owner should definitely be a lover of the outdoors.

KEY TO CHARACTER	
INTELLIGENCE	****
TEMPERAMENT	****
EASE OF COAT CARE	**
SUITABILITY FOR SMALL DWELLING	*
***** (5) = VERY GOOD	

BRITISH KENNEL CLUB STANDARD

SPANIEL (IRISH WATER)

CHARACTERISTICS. — The gait, peculiar to the breed, differs from that of any other variety of Spaniel.

GENERAL APPEARANCE. — The Irish Water Spaniel is a gundog bred for work in all types of shooting, and particularly suited for wild-fowling. His fitness for this purpose should be evident in his appearance; he is a strongly built, compact dog, intelligent, enduring and eager.

Head and Skull. — The head should be of good size. The skull high in dome, of good length and width sufficient to allow adequate brain capacity. The muzzle long, strong and somewhat square with a gradual stop. The face should be smooth and the skull covered with long curls in the form of a ponounced topknot growing in a well-defined peak to a point between the eyes. Nose large and well developed, dark liver colour. With all there should be an impression of fineness.

Eyes. — Comparatively small, medium to dark-brown colour, bright and alert.

Ears. — Very long and lobe-shaped in the leather, low set, hanging close to the cheeks and covered with long twisted curls of live hair.

Mouth. — The jaws should be strong, with a perfect regular and complete scissor bite, i.e., the upper teeth closely overlapping the lower teeth and set square to the jaws.

Neck. — strongly set into the shoulders, powerful, arching and long enough to carry the head well above the level of the back. The back and sides of the neck should be covered with curls similar to those on the body. The throat should be smooth, the smooth hair forming a V-shaped patch from the back of the lower jaw to the breast bone.

Forequarters. — The shoulders should be powerful and sloping. The chest deep and of large girth with ribs so well sprung behind the shoulders as to give a barrel-shaped appearance to the body but with normal width and curvature between the forelegs. The forelegs should be well boned and straight, with arms well let down and carrying the forearm at elbow and knee in a straight line with the point of the shoulder.

Body. — should be of good size. The back short, broad and level, strongly coupled to the hind quarters. The ribs carried well back. The loins deep and wide. The body as a whole being so proportioned as to give a barrel-shaped appearance accentuated by the springing of the ribs.

Hindquarters. — Powerful with long well-bent stifles and hocks set low.

Feet. — Should be large and somewhat round and spreading; well-covered with hair over and between the toes.

Tail. — Peculiar to the breed, should be short and straight, thick at the root and tapering to a fine point. It should be low set, carried straight and below the level of the back; and in length should not reach the hock joint. Three to four inches of the tail at the root should be covered by close curls which stop abruptly, the remainder should be bare or covered by straight fine hairs.

Coat. — Should be composed of dense, tight, crisp ringlets free from woolliness. The hair should have a natural oiliness. The forelegs covered with feather in curls or ringlets down to the feet. The feather should be abundant all round, though shorter in front so as only to give a rough appearance. Below the hocks the hindlegs should be smooth in front, but feathered behind down to the feet.

Colour. — A rich dark liver having the purplish tint or bloom peculiar to the breed and sometimes referred to as puce-liver.

Weight and Size. — Height to the shoulders: Dogs about 53 to 59cm (21″ to 23″). Bitches about 51 to 56cm (20″ to 22″).

Note. — Male animals should have two apparently normal testicles fully descended into the scrotum.

MAIN AMERICAN KENNEL CLUB VARIATION TO STANDARD FOR THE IRISH WATER SPANIEL —

Height and Weight. — dogs, 22 to 24 inches; bitches, 21 to 23 inches. Dogs, 55 to 65 pounds; bitches, 45 to 58 pounds.

IRISH WATER SPANIEL REGISTRATIONS 1981 — 87 INCLUSIVE

1981 — 98
1982 — 83
1983 — 117
1984 — 115
1985 — 122
1986 — 170
1987 — 144

YET TO WIN CRUFTS BEST-IN-SHOW.

SUSSEX SPANIEL

The Sussex Spaniel is one of the stockier of the Spaniel group and also one of the rarest. He goes back to the late eighteenth century and owes his early development to a breeder in Sussex called Fuller. Even then numbers were few and the Sussex Spaniel has often verged on extinction. Fortunately such features as his beautiful colour and handsomeness, coupled with renowned working ability in the field, have ensured that he has always kept a small yet devoted following.

Although not the speediest of the gun dogs, the Sussex has excellent stamina and stubbornly refuses to be thwarted by dense undergrowth in his search for prey. His luxurious coat is also an advantage when working amongst thorns and the like.

This is a breed of great beauty and the unique golden liver colour of the coat is a marvellous sight on a well groomed dog. He is as amiable as his kind facial expression would suggest and a commendable companion for someone who leads life at a leisurely pace. Exercise, however is important and walks of a fair length will be enjoyed by the Sussex. He is very even tempered and will prove easily house trained and loyal to his owner.

```
┌─────────────────────────────────────────────────────┐
│              KEY TO CHARACTER                         │
├─────────────────────────────────────────────────────┤
│                                                       │
│   INTELLIGENCE              ****                       │
│                                                       │
│   TEMPERAMENT               *****                      │
│                                                       │
│   EASE OF COAT CARE         **                         │
│                                                       │
│   SUITABILITY FOR           *                          │
│   SMALL DWELLING                                      │
│                                                       │
├─────────────────────────────────────────────────────┤
│            ***** (5) = VERY GOOD                       │
└─────────────────────────────────────────────────────┘
```

BRITISH KENNEL CLUB STANDARD

SPANIEL (SUSSEX)

GENERAL APPEARANCE. — Massive and strongly built. An active, energetic, strong dog, whose characteristic movement is a decided roll, and unlike that of any other Spaniel.

Head and Skull. — The skull should be wide and show a moderate curve from ear to ear, neither flat nor apple headed, with a centre indentation and a pronounced stop. Brows frowning — occiput decided, but not pointed. Nostrils well developed and liver colour. A well balanced head.

Eyes. — Hazel colour, fairly large, not too full, but soft expression and not showing the haw over much.

Ears. — Thick, fairly large and lobe shape, set moderately low but above eye level. Should lie closely, hair soft and wavy, but not too profuse.

Mouth. — Strong and level, neither over nor undershot, with a scissor bite.

Neck. — Long, strong and slightly arched, not carrying the head much above the level of the back. Not much throatiness, but well marked frill.

Forequarters. — The shoulders should be sloping and free; arms well boned as well as muscular. Knees large and strong, pasterns short and well boned. Legs rather short and strong, moderately well feathered.

Body. — Chest deep and well developed; not too round and wide. Back and loin well developed and muscular both in width and depth. The back ribs must be deep. Whole body should be strong and level with no sign of waistiness from aitches to hips.

Hindquarters. — The thighs must be strongly boned as well as muscular; hocks large and strong, legs rather short and strong with good bone, moderately well feathered. The hind legs should not appear shorter than the fore legs, or be too much bent at the hocks so as to give a settery appearance, which is objectionable. The hind legs should be well feathered above the hocks, but not much hair below the hocks.

Feet. — Circular, well padded, well feathered between toes.

Tail. — Set low and not carried above level of the back. Free actioned, thickly clothed with hair, but no feather. Docked from 5 to 7 inches.

Coat. — Abundant and flat with no tendency to curl and ample undercoat for weather resistance.

Colour. — Rich golden liver and hair shading to gold at the tips: the gold predominating. Dark liver or puce is objectionable.

Weight and Size. — Ideal weight: Dogs 20.4Kg (45 lbs). Bitches 18.2Kg (40 lbs). Height 38 to 41cm (15″ to 16″).

Note. — Male animals should have two apparently normal testicles fully descended into the scrotum.

MAIN AMERICAN KENNEL CLUB VARIATION TO STANDARD FOR THE SUSSEX SPANIEL —

Weight — From 35 pounds to 45 pounds.

SUSSEX SPANIEL REGISTRATIONS 1981 — 87 INCLUSIVE

1981 —	55
1982 —	82
1983 —	62
1984 —	80
1985 —	93
1986 —	102
1987 —	75

YET TO WIN CRUFTS BEST-IN-SHOW.

WELSH SPRINGER SPANIEL

There is some debate as to which of the two Springer Spaniel breeds is the oldest. Some maintain that this honour goes to the Welsh variety, but most believe that the English Springer was crossed with other Spaniels to produce his smaller cousin. Nonetheless, this is a breed of many years standing, having been registered in 1902 and has a fine reputation amongst Welsh shooting enthusiasts. Although not quite as hardy as the English Springer, he thoroughly enjoys field work and his devotees will testify that he enjoys all aspects of it.

He can be a little scatter-brained at times and correct training, either for sport or general obedience is essential to allow his many good qualities to shine through.

If kept well groomed, which is not an enormous task, the rich red and white coat can be a superb sight. His head and muzzle are shaped slightly differently from the English Springer, but his facial expression is just as endearing.

Like all sporting dogs, maximum mental and physical condition can only be achieved through lengthy exercise each day. A prospective owner must prepare for this as the Welsh Springer Spaniel will be full of running long after his owner has tired.

This is a breed to be recommended to anyone who is seeking a loyal, affectionate, medium-sized dog for their home.

KEY TO CHARACTER	
INTELLIGENCE	****
TEMPERAMENT	****
EASE OF COAT CARE	***
SUITABILITY FOR SMALL DWELLING	**
***** (5) = VERY GOOD	

BRITISH KENNEL CLUB STANDARD

SPANIEL (WELSH SPRINGER)

CHARACTERISTICS. — The "Welsh Spaniel" or "Springer" is also known and referred to in Wales as a "Starter". He is of very ancient and pure origin, and is a distinct variety.

GENERAL APPEARANCE. — A symmetrical, compact, strong, merry, very active dog; not stilty; obviously built for endurance and hard work. A quick and active mover displaying plenty of push and drive.

Head and Skull. — Skull proportionate, of moderate length, slightly domed, with clearly defined stop and well chiselled below the eyes. Muzzle of medium length, straight, fairly square; the nostrils well developed and flesh-coloured or dark. A short chubby head is objectionable.

Eyes. — Hazel or dark, medium size, not prominent, nor sunken, nor showing haw.

Ears. — Set moderately low and hanging close to the cheeks, comparatively small and gradually narrowing towards the tip and shaped somewhat like a vine leaf, covered with setter-like feathering.

Mouth. — The jaws should be strong, with a perfect regular and complete scissor bite, i.e., the upper teeth closely overlapping the lower teeth and set square to the jaws.

Neck. — Long and muscular, clean in throat, neatly set into long, sloping shoulders.

Forequarters. — Forelegs of medium length, straight, well boned, moderately feathered.

Body. — Not long; strong and muscular with deep brisket, well-sprung ribs; length of body should be proportionate to length of leg, and very well balanced; muscular loins lightly arched and well coupled up.

Hindquarters. — Strong and muscular, wide and fully developed with deep second thighs. Hind legs well boned, hocks well let down; stifles moderately bent (neither turned in nor out), moderately feathered.

Feet. — Round, with thick pads. Firm and cat-like, not too large or spreading.

Tail. — Well set on and low, never carried above the level of the back; lightly feathered and lively in action.

Coat. — Straight or flat, of a nice silky texture, never wiry nor wavy. A curly coat is most objectionable.

Colour. — Rich red and white only.

Weight and Size. — A dog not to exceed 48cm (19″) in height at shoulder and a bitch 46cm (18″) approximately.

Faults. — Any departure form the foregoing points should be considered a fault and the seriousness of the fault should be in exact proportion to its degree.

Note. — Male animals should have two apparently normal testicles fully descended into the scrotum.

WELSH SPRINGER SPANIEL REGISTRATIONS 1981 — 87 INCLUSIVE

1981 — 596
1982 — 670
1983 — 710
1984 — 648
1985 — 702
1986 — 715
1987 — 528

YET TO WIN CRUFTS BEST-IN-SHOW.

WEIMARANER

The "grey ghost" as this breed is often nicknamed, has one of the strangest and some might say of of the most attractive colourations of all breeds. The slick, gleaming coat gives a steely appearance which is all the more striking on a muscualr dog such as the Weimaraner.

Officially recognised in his native Germany in the nineteenth century, the Weimaraner has been perfected over a period of many years. A type of German Bloodhound known as a Schweisshund was one of his main ancestors and as is plain to see by the Weimaraner's overall shape, Pointer blood was also introduced.

The Germans had been seeking to develop the ultimate gun dog and it was the court of Weimar which pursued this task with the greatest vigour. the early Weimaraners were referred to as Weimar hounds or Weimar Pointers and were used to hunt big game when it was abundant in Germany. Later, of course, the huntsmen had to be content with bird and small game and the Weimaraner excelled at this work.

German breeding was very secretive and disciplined and it was not until the late 1920's that specimens were allowed into the U.S.A., a nation which has taken a great liking to the Weimaraner. It was to be another thirty years before the breed reached Britain and numbers are now steadily on the increase.

The Weimaraner is a dog of good learning capacity with a lively and friendly disposition. They are one of the foremost sporting dogs in the world so exercise should be of paramount importance with lots of free running. Generally he lives very happily in the home environment but, his exuberant nature should be tempered by firm and careful training when young.

KEY TO CHARACTER	
INTELLIGENCE	****
TEMPERAMENT	****
EASE OF COAT CARE	*****
SUITABILITY FOR SMALL DWELLING	*
***** (5) = VERY GOOD	

BRITISH KENNEL CLUB STANDARD

WEIMARANER

CHARACTERISTICS. — In the case of the Weimaraner his hunting ability is the paramount concern and any fault of body or mind which detracts from this ability should be penalised. The dog should display a temperament that is fearless, friendly, protective and obedient.

GENERAL APPEARANCE. — A medium sized grey dog with light eyes, he should present a picture of great driving power, stamina, alertness and balance. Above all, the dog should indicate ability to work hard in the field. Movement should be effortless and ground-covering and should indicate smooth co-ordination. When seen from the rear, the hind feet should parallel the front feet. When seen from the side, the top line should remain strong and level.

Head and Skull. — Moderately long and aristocratic, with moderate stop and slight median line extending back over the forehead. Rather prominent occipital bone and ears set well back. Measurement from the top of the nose to stop to equal that from the stop to the occipital prominence. The flews should be moderately deep, enclosing a powerful jaw. Foreface perfectly straight, delicate at the nostrils. Skin tightly drawn. Neck clean cut and moderately long. Expression keen, kind and intelligent.

Eyes. — Medium-sized in shades of amber or blue-grey, not protruding or too deeply set, placed far enough apart to indicate good disposition and intelligence. When dilated under excitement the eyes may appear almost black.

Ears. — Long and lobular, slightly folded and set high. The ear when drawn alongside the jaw should end approximately one inch from the point of the nose.

Mouth. — Well-set, strong and even teeth, well developed and proportionate to jaw with correct scissor bite (the upper teeth protruding slightly over the lower teeth). Complete dentition is greatly desired. grey nose, lips and gums of pinkish flesh shade.

Forequarters. — Forelegs straight and strong, with measurement from elbow to the ground equalling the distance from the elbow to the top of the withers.

Body. — The length of the body from the highest point of the withers to the root of the tail should equal the measurement from the highest point of the withers to the ground. The top line should be level with a slightly sloping croup. The chest should be well developed and deep, shoulders well laid and snug. Ribs well sprung and long. Abdomen firmly held, moderately tucked up flank. The brisket should drop to the elbow.

Hindquarters. — Moderately angulated with well turned stifle. The hock joint well let down and tuned neither in nor out. Musculation well developed.

Feet. — Firm and compact. Toes well arched, pads closed and thick. Nails short and grey or amber in colour. Dew claws allowable only on imported dogs.

Tail. — Docked at a point such that the tail remaining shall just cover the scrotum in dogs and vulva in bitches. The thickness of the tail should be in proportion to the body and it should be carried in a manner expressing confidence and sound temperament. In the long-haired Weimaraner the tip of the tail should be removed.

Coat. — Short, smooth and sleek. In the long-haired Weimaraner the coat should be form 1-2 inches long on the body and somewhat longer on the neck, chest and belly. The tail and the backs of the limbs should be feathered.

Colour. — Preferably silver grey, shades of mouse or roe grey are admissible. The colour usually blends to a lighter shade on head and ears. A dark eel stripe frequently occurs along the back. The whole coat gives an appearance of metallic sheen. Small white mark allowable on chest but not on any other part of the body. White spots that have resulted from injuries should not be penalised. Colour of the long-haired Weimaraner as the short-haired.

Size. — Height at withers. Dogs 61 to 69cm (24″ to 27″), bitches 56 to 64cm (22″ to 25″).

Faults. — Shyness or viciousness. Any colour or marking other than specified in this Standard.

Note. — Male animals should have two apparently normal testicles fully descended into the scrotum.

MAIN AMERICAN KENNEL CLUB VARIATION TO STANDARD FOR THE WEIMARANER —

Height. — Height at the withers: Dogs, 25 to 27 inches; bitches, 23 to 25 inches.

WEIMARANER REGISTRATIONS 1981 — 87 INCLUSIVE

1981 — 671
1982 — 735
1983 — 845
1984 — 893
1985 — 1070
1986 — 1307
1987 — 1283

YET TO WIN CRUFTS BEST-IN-SHOW.